EARTH

Gabrielle Woolfitt

Wayland

Titles in this series
Air
Earth
Fire
Water

TOPIC CHART

	SCIENCE*	ENGLISH	TECHNOLOGY	GEOGRAPHY	HISTORY	PHYSICAL EDUCATION	MUSIC	ART	RELIGIOUS EDUCATION
What is Earth?	AT 2 L2–4								
The planet Earth	AT 4 L2–5			AT 1 L5	AT 1 L3				
Earth power	AT 4 L2–5								
Earthquakes				AT 3 L4					
Rocks and landscapes	AT 3 L2–5			AT 3 L4					
Creation of Earth		AT 2 L2–5			AT 2 L2–4				✔
Earth stories		AT 1 L2–3 ATS 2,3 L2–5							
Earth art				AT 2 L2				✔	
Earth buildings	AT 3 L2–4		AT 1 L4 AT 4 L3–5		AT 1 L2–4 AT 3 L2–5				
Soil	AT 2 L2–5 AT 3 L4			AT 5 L2–3					
Burrowing in earth	AT 2 L2–4						✔		
Earth sports				AT 2 L1		✔			
Model of the Earth			AT 3 L2–5	AT 1 L3					
Earthguide		ALL ATS L2–5	AT 3 L2–5 AT 4 L2–5	ALL ATS L2–5	AT 2 L2–5			✔	

KEY AT = Attainment Target L = Level *Proposed ATs, October 1991

First published in 1992 by
Wayland (Publishers) Ltd
61 Western Road, Hove
East Sussex BN3 1JD, England

© Copyright 1992 Wayland (Publishers) Ltd

Editor: Cath Senker
Designer: Helen White
Consultant: Tom Collins,
Deputy Headmaster of St Leonards
CEP School, East Sussex

British Library Cataloguing in Publication Data

Woolfitt, Gabrielle
Earth. – (The elements)
I. Title II. Series
550

ISBN 0 7502 0380 3

Typeset by White Design
Cover and inside artwork by Maureen Jackson
Printed by G. Canale & C.S.p.A. Turin
Bound in France by A.G.M.

CONTENTS

Words printed in **bold** are explained in the glossary.

WHAT IS EARTH?

ABOVE **Every person on the Earth is different from all the others. But we all need the same things to stay alive.**

Earth is the name of our planet. There are more than 5,000,000,000 (five billion) people living on the Earth and they are all different! There are millions of different kinds of animals and plants as well.

All living things rely on the special water and air system which the Earth provides. Many living things suffer when people do not take care of the Earth.

Here are some of the ways that living things use the Earth:

Plants grow roots deep into the earth. The roots collect water and hold the plants upright.

Animals make burrows underground. The burrows are safe places to keep their young.

People dig down into the Earth to find precious metals, like gold, and important fuels, such as coal.

Can you think of other ways that we use the Earth? Do you think that people could live in a **space station** instead of on the Earth?

BELOW **Here is the Earth, seen from space. Which continents can you see?**

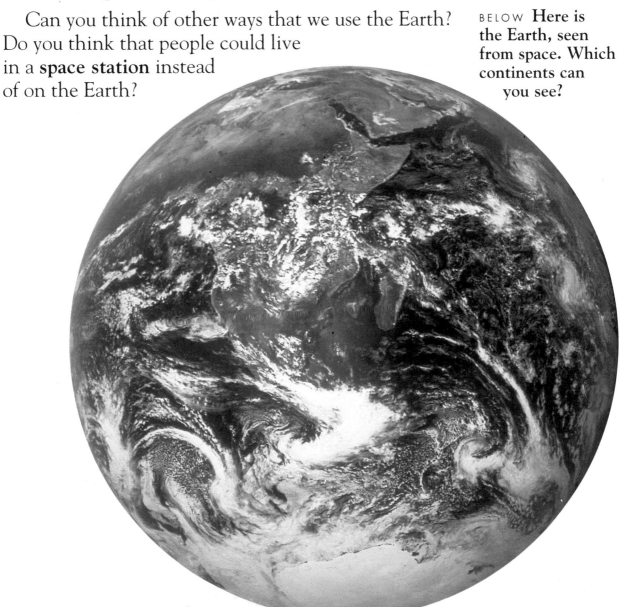

THE PLANET EARTH

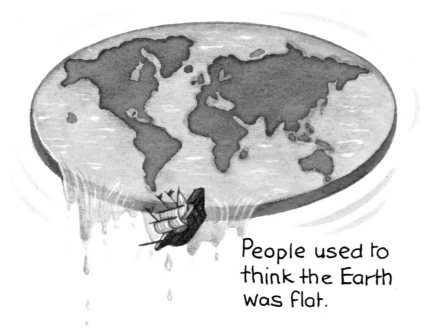

People used to think the Earth was flat.

The Earth is an enormous **sphere**, spinning in space like a big blue ball. The Earth is about 39,000 km (24,000 miles) all the way round. It would take you a whole year to walk around the Earth without stopping!

The Earth takes 24 hours to turn all the way round. When your part of the Earth first points towards the Sun, it is morning. Throughout the day the Earth continues to turn. When your part of the Earth turns away from the Sun, it is night. On the other side of the world, people are waking up as you go to bed.

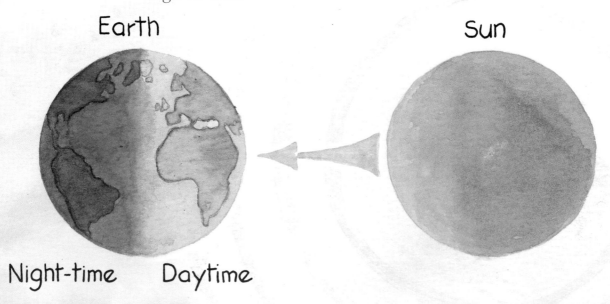

Earth

Sun

Night-time   Daytime

Find your country on a map of the world. Now have a look at your country on a globe. Is it exactly the same shape? **Compare** some other countries on the map and on the globe. Which countries stay the same shape? Which countries are changed the most?

Do you think a globe or a map gives a better picture of the Earth?

ABOVE **These children are trying to find their country on a globe.**

EARTH POWER

ABOVE **Far away from the Earth, this astronaut feels very little gravity. He can float in space and he feels weightless.**

The pull of the Earth is called gravity. Gravity is a force that pulls everything towards the Earth's centre. You stay on the Earth because gravity holds you there. If there were no gravity you would float up into space!

When you jump up into the air you go against gravity. Gravity pulls you back down to Earth again. Work out how to measure how high you can jump.

The core of the Earth is made mainly of liquid iron. Iron is **magnetic**. The Earth acts like a giant magnet. It has a north and a south pole, like every magnet. The place called the North Pole is near the magnetic north pole.

People cannot feel magnetism but some animals can. Birds use the Earth's **magnetic field** to sense which way to fly when they **migrate** between their summer and winter homes.

BELOW **These birds migrate together in a flock.**

EARTHQUAKES

Earthquakes make the ground shake. Powerful earthquakes can split the ground apart. An earthquake under the sea can make giant waves. Many people may die when these things happen.

The more energy an earthquake has, the more damage it can do. The **Richter scale** is used to measure how powerful earthquakes are. This table will give you a rough idea of the Richter scale.

Number on Richter scale and what happens

1 too weak to notice

2 the floor moves slightly

3 parked cars move a little

4 plaster cracks

5 weak buildings are damaged people are frightened

6 difficult for people to stand up ordinary buildings are damaged

7 ground cracks and well-built buildings are destroyed

8 most buildings are destroyed large waves at sea

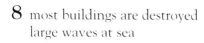

9 huge damage

Only a few walls were left standing after an earthquake hit this part of Armenia. The dog is helping to find people buried in the rubble.

A very big earthquake hit San Francisco, USA, in 1906. Hundreds of people were killed. Nowadays, buildings in San Francisco are **constructed** in special ways so that they are less likely to fall down when there is an earthquake.

In many countries there is no special planning to protect people from earthquakes. One of the strongest earthquakes ever recorded was in Armenia in 1988. Tens of thousands of people died in the disaster.

Find out why earthquakes are more likely to happen in some parts of the world than others.

ROCKS AND LANDSCAPES

ABOVE **These amazing rocks are in Arizona, USA. They were shaped by wind blowing sand against the rocks and wearing away the sides.**

There are many kinds of rock, formed in different ways.

Deep inside the Earth the rocks are so hot that they have melted. Some of this hot, liquid rock comes to the surface when there is an earthquake or a volcano. When it cools and hardens, it is called igneous rock.

Another kind of rock is made from broken pieces of material, including sand, and very small animals that have died. The sand and animal remains build up in layers at the bottom of rivers and seas.

When each new layer is added, the layers underneath become squashed. After millions of years these layers turn into **sedimentary rock**.

The surface of the Earth is covered in hills and valleys, tall mountains and wide plains. All these kinds of landscape have taken thousands of years to form. Sometimes forces inside the Earth push layers of rocks up, and into folds. This makes mountains.

Water and wind gradually wear away the sides of valleys. Rivers carry soil from fields down towards the sea. Look at some photographs of different kinds of landscapes. Find out how the shapes were formed.

BELOW **This is a U-shaped valley in Scotland. The shape was carved out by a huge river of ice many thousands of years ago. A small river still flows along the bottom.**

CREATION OF EARTH

How did the Earth come into being? Where did life come from? People have always wanted to know the answer to these questions. Most peoples of the world have a **creation** story.

The Tiwi, one of the Aboriginal peoples from Australia, say the world was sung into being during Dreamtime:

Before the first sunrise, all was darkness. The Earth was flat and featureless. Then an old blind woman, Mudungkala, rose miraculously out of the ground, carrying in her arms a boy and two girls. Before Mudungkala left she covered the bare land with plants and animals so that people would have food and shelter.

BELOW **Poles like these are used by the Tiwi at important events, like funerals. People act out the creation story.**

This is how the Book of Genesis, in the Bible, explains how God created the Earth:

In the beginning of creation, when God made Heaven and Earth, the Earth was without form and void, with darkness over the face of the abyss, and a mighty wind that swept over the surface of the waters.

Scientists believe that the **solar system** was made from space dust and gas, called a nebula. About 4,600 million years ago, the nebula began to shrink, forming the Sun and planets. Nobody really knows how the Earth was formed.

ABOVE **This stained glass window shows God creating the birds and the animals.**

EARTH ART

Have you ever written your name in the sand on a beach and watched as the sea washes it away? If you have, then you are an earth artist.

You could make pictures using leaves and flowers. Arrange some pebbles to make an interesting pattern. Weave a plait of long grasses. Build a pile of stones on a hillside. These are all kinds of earth art because you are using natural materials.

Sand painting is a special form of earth art. Native American doctors used sand paintings to heal people. After **diagnosing** an illness the doctor would decide on the right painting to cure it. The painting told a story.

The doctor made the painting by pouring sand out of his hand. He added different colours until a clear picture could be seen. When the picture was finished the person would start to feel better.

ABOVE RIGHT **This blanket has a sand painting pattern. Can you see the two gods, a maize plant, and a rainbow around the edge?**
LEFT **This stone sculpture is in Harare, Zimbabwe.**

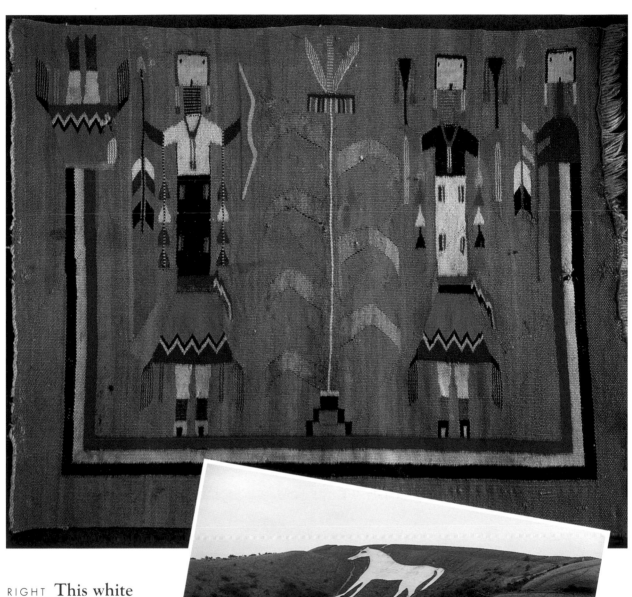

RIGHT This white horse was carved on to a hillside in Wiltshire, England. The hill is made from chalk. When the grass is cut away you can see the horse from many kilometres away.

EARTH BUILDINGS

Materials from the Earth are used in many kinds of building.

Stone is a very good building material. It is **quarried** from the ground. Blocks of stone are cut to shape, and fitted together. Sometimes they are stuck in place with **cement**.

This is the Acropolis in Greece. It is an enormous temple made of stone. It was built nearly 2,000 years ago and it is still standing today.

Do you live in an old building, or is there one near your home? When was it built? What is it made from?

Wood is often used for building. Wood comes from trees that grow on the Earth.

In many places, buildings are constructed from bricks. Bricks are made from a soft rock called clay. The clay is cut and shaped. Then it is put into tins and baked – like baking bread!

What other building materials do you know? Where do they come from? Make a poster to show what you have found out about buildings.

SOIL

Take a handful of soil. What does it feel like? Can you tell what it is made from by looking at it? Spread it out on a sheet of newspaper and look at it closely with a magnifying glass.

You should see some minibeasts crawling around in your soil. Do you know what they are? There will be bits of dead plants and animals rotting in the soil. They turn into a substance called humus, which makes the soil more **fertile**. Do you know of some other ways of making soil fertile?

Soil is made from crumbs of rock, mixed with humus, water and air. Big crumbs of rock make a sandy soil. Small crumbs make clay.

Plants need water and chemicals from the soil to grow. Plan an experiment to grow seeds in different soils. Find out which soil is best for each kind of seed.

ABOVE **This girl is planting onions in Rajasthan, India.**

BURROWING IN EARTH

Mud! Mud! Glorious mud!
Nothing quite like it for cooling the blood.
So follow me, follow!
Down to the hollow
And there let us wallow in glorious mud.

This is part of the *Hippopotamuses' Song.*
Hippopotamuses live mainly in rivers and **swamps**.
These ones are cooling down by taking a mud bath.

BELOW
Hippopotamuses are so heavy that they find it quite hard to climb out of the mud!

Have you ever watched a bird taking a sand bath? The sand helps the bird to clean between its feathers.

Can you think of some animals that make their homes out of rock or earth?

Some birds build their nests on to the side of a cliff using mud.

Many animals dig their homes underground. Rabbits live in burrows, and so do worms. Badgers live in burrows called sets.

Find out about some other burrowing animals that make their homes in the earth.

ABOVE **These young rabbits have been outside the burrow with their mother. If there is danger they can quickly go underground for safety.**

EARTH SPORTS

Walking is a good way to enjoy the countryside. You can see many kinds of scenery and look out for different plants and animals.

In a town there is not much open space. In the country you will find beautiful scenery. The fresh air will make you feel healthy. You could take a picnic. Or you could be more energetic and try hill-walking.

BELOW **These people are enjoying a walk along the rocks at Peggy's Cove in Nova Scotia, Canada.**

LEFT **Rock climbing is a dangerous and exciting sport. This woman is fixing a rope to the rock. If she slips, the rope will stop her falling.**

You must always go walking with an adult. Never go alone. Check the forecast to make sure the weather will be fine. Look at a map to decide which **route** to follow, and work out how long the walk will take you.

Take the map, some food and drink, and a waterproof coat. When you feel more confident you can plan a longer walk.

Other kinds of earth sports include caving and rock climbing. If you want to try these activities you need to join a club and learn how to do them safely.

ACTIVITIES

Make a model of the inside of the Earth.
The inside of the Earth is made up of four layers. It has a thin skin, called the crust, which is hard and wrinkled. This is the part that we live on.

Next there is a hot, solid layer, called the mantle. Then there is the outer core which is made of very hot, molten iron. In the centre of the Earth there is a solid mass, which is probably a heavy lump of iron.

1. Cut a section out of a large, plain plastic ball.
2. Stuff the inside with balls of screwed-up newspaper.
3. Cut out a circle of paper and paint it to show the four inside layers.
4. Fold the paper in half and fit it in the open part of the ball.
5. Decorate the outside of the ball to show the crust, with the oceans and continents on it. Use modelling clay or coloured paper shapes.

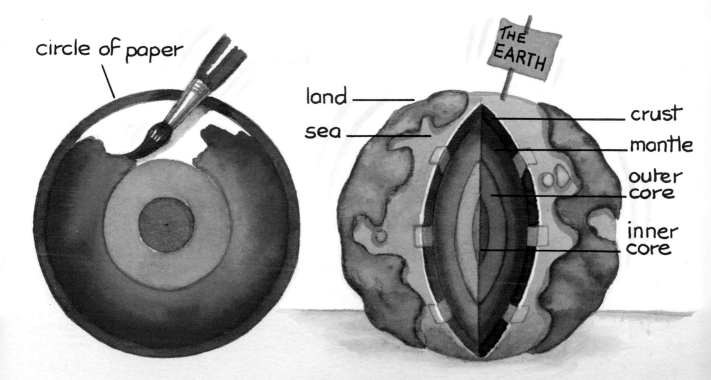

Make an Earthguide.

Imagine that some people from another planet are coming to visit. Make a guide to Earth that will help them.

Decide what they will need to know. You could describe the forms of life on Earth. What grows here? Talk about the different kinds of food that Earth people eat, and the music that they listen to. You might want to talk about the problems on Earth, such as pollution and hunger.

Use photographs from magazines and draw your own pictures. Type the words on a computer. Paste the words and pictures on to thick paper and work out the best way of fixing the sheets together.

These girls are making some pages about life on Earth as part of their Earthguide.

GLOSSARY

Cement   A mixture of clay and limestone used in building.
Compare   To see what is the same and what is different about two things.
Constructed   Built.
Creation   The act of making or inventing something.
Diagnosing   Working out what illness someone has.
Fertile   Full of goodness so that many plants can grow.
Magnetic   Able to attract other materials towards it.
Magnetic field   The area of attraction around a magnet.
Migrate   To move to live in another place for a while, as birds do at certain times of the year.
Quarried   Cut or blasted out of a large, open pit.
Richter scale   The scale used to measure the power of earthquakes. Each level on the scale is ten times more powerful than the one before.
Route   A way or road from one place to another.
Sedimentary rock   The rock that is formed when layers of sand, pebbles and animal remains are squashed for millions of years.
Solar system   The Sun and all the planets and moons that move around it.
Space station   A space machine that can stay in space for a long time with people in it.
Sphere   Something that is completely round in shape, like a ball.
Swamp   An area of wet, soft ground.

FINDING OUT MORE

Books
The Earth by Wendy Baker (Two-Can Publishing, 1992)
Earthquake by John Dudman (Wayland, 1992)
Janice Van Cleave's Earth Science for Every Kid by Van Cleave and Janice Pratt (Wiley Inc., 1991)
Planet Earth by Mark Pettigrew (Franklin Watts, 1990)
1000 Facts about the Earth (Kingfisher Books, 1991)

Computer software
Landscapes and People Today by CDG (Scotland) Ltd, PO Box 238, Glasgow G44 3LX, Scotland
Natural History by Kosmos Software Ltd, 1 Pilgrim Close, Harlington, Dunstable, Beds LUX 6LX, England

Music
The Creation by Haydn

Poetry
The Last Rabbit ed. Jennifer Curry (Mammoth, 1990)
What on Earth? Poems with a Conservation Theme ed. Judith Nicholls (Faber, 1989)

Teachers' resources
Down to Earth by Don Nelson (Crucible Books, 1990)
Rocks and Fossils, Art and Craft Design and Technology magazine (Scholastic, February 1991)
Sun, Moon, and Stars, Science Mini Unit (Scholastic, 1991)

INDEX

Page numbers in **bold** indicate subjects shown in pictures, but not mentioned in the text on those pages.

Picture Acknowledgements
The publishers would like to thank the following for allowing their illustrations to be used in this book: Bridgeman Art Library 15; British Film Institute 16, 17; Chapel Studios 26; Eye Ubiquitous (Redmayne) 21, (Bouineau) 23; Frank Spooner Pictures (Shone) 11; Northern Territory Tourist Commission 14; Oxford Scientific Films *cover*, (Bernard) 25; Topham 8; Wayland Picture Library 18, (A. Blackburn) 7, 22, 29; Werner Forman Archive 19 (above); ZEFA 4, 5, (Mueller) 9, (Damm) 12, 13, 19, (Damm) 20, (Paysan) 24, 27.